Stopping points during the tour:

D0817780

PICTURE CREDITS

Albertina, Wien: p. 25 b.

Bayer. Staatsgemäldesammlungen, Alte Pinakothek, München: p. 26 b.

Germanisches Nationalmuseum Nürnberg: p. 9, 23 b., 31, 32, 64 b., 65.

Geschichte Für Alle e.V. – Institut für Regionalgeschichte: p. 4, 5, 6, 8, 12 t., 16 o., 22, 26 o., 28, 32 o., 36, 40 o., 42 o., 48, 52 o., 56 o., 57, 60 o., 61 b., 62 t., 64 t.

Industrie- und Handelskammer Nürnberg: p. 40, 41.

Museen der Stadt Nürnberg: p. 25 t., 37, 42/43 b., 45, 66, 67 t. (Photographer: Mario Gastinger), 67 b., 68, 69 (Photographer: Herbert Liedel).

Museen der Stadt Nürnberg, Graphische Sammlung: p. 11, 15, 17, 21, 23 t., 27, 33, 46, 49 t., 51, 53, 55, 59 t., 62.

Oerter, Fritz Henry: p. 20.

Privat: p. 16 b.

St. Klara Nürnberg: p. 63 t.

St. Lorenz Nürnberg: p. 3, 56 b., 58, 59 b.

St. Sebald Nürnberg: p. 34, 35, 44.

Staatsarchiv Nürnberg: p. 12 b., 13, 19, 49 b.

Stadt Nürnberg, Presse- und Informationsamt: p. 47.

Stadtarchiv Nürnberg: p. 9, 10, 14, 18, 38, 39 b., 50, 52 b., 53 b., 54, 60 b., 61 t., 63 b.

Stadtbibliothek Nürnberg: p. 7, 24, 29, 30, 39 t., 43 t.

right: The oldest painting of the city of Nuremberg is located in the choir of St. Lawrence's Church. It forms the background scene for the central section of the so-called Krellscher Altar. The work shows the city viewed from the west and places it in an idyllic landscape. The new city wall has already been completed. Oil painting on wood, 1483.

SANDBERG VERLAG

© Sandberg Verlag
Wiesentalstraße 32
90419 Nürnberg

Information in English available at:
www.geschichte-fuer-alle.de

info@geschichte-fuer-alle.de
Phone +49-911-307360
Fax +49-911-3073616

Designer: Norbert Kühlthau, Nuremberg
Printing: Verlagsdruckerei Schmidt, Neustadt/A

Nuremberg 2009

ISBN 978-3-930699-59-9 (English)
ISBN 978-3-930699-58-2 (German)

Martin Schieber

NUREMBERG THE MEDIEVAL CITY

A Short Guide

Translated by John Jenkins

Historic Walks 6

Published by
Geschichte Für Alle e.V. – Institut für Regionalgeschichte

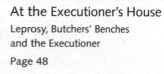
Chapter |

Nuremberg
The Medieval City

Walking Through History

■ Nuremberg was one of the most important cities in the Holy Roman Empire. Just before that empire ended, tourists began to show great interest in the ambience associated with the Middle Ages and as a result, the romantic view of Nuremberg was born. The rapid growth in tourism consolidated the city's reputation as the "treasure chest of the German Empire" and Dürer's city became the epitome of medieval Germany. Richard Wagner's "The Mastersingers of Nuremberg" constitutes one of the peaks in this development.

The fact that Nuremberg became the leading industrial metropolis in Bavaria in the 19th century was willingly suppressed. Symptomatic in this regard is Hermann Hesse's "Nuremberg Journey" from 1927. Hesse, seeking Romanticism, was appalled by the frantic pace of the modern city. A few years, later the National Socialists cleverly integrated the old town into the propaganda of their Party rallies. The end for medieval Nuremberg appeared to have arrived on January 2nd 1945 – it lay in ruins after Allied bombers had destroyed more than 90 percent of the old city.

The careful and at the same time committed reconstruction was orientated towards retaining the city structure that had grown up over the years. Consequently, despite everything that it had lost, Nuremberg remained a first-class destination for tourists. Between the imperial castle and the New Museum you can discover a wealth of medieval art, while the city wall, the Hospital of the Holy Spirit, the town hall and the splendid churches tell the story of the inhabitants of Nuremberg and their lives in the imperial city.

Since 1985 History for Everyone (Geschichte Für Alle e.V.) has been offering a variety of thematic tours in the old city and this short guide contains the essence, as it were, of those trips through Nuremberg. We look forward to meeting you personally on one of our guided tours.

Martin Schieber
Geschichte Für Alle e.V. –
Institute for Regional History
Nuremberg, October 2009

①

The Freedom (Freiung) Area

View over the City

This bird's eye view of Nuremberg by Wenzel Hollar, a student of the painter Merian, shows the layout of the old city after its final expansion. The winding lanes of the first settlement, between the castle and St. Sebaldus' Church in the northwest, are clearly visible, in contrast to the more systematic arrangement of the streets in the St. Lawrence settlement in the south. Coloured copper engraving, 1654.

■ On reaching the castle walls in the area known as the Burgfreiung, the visitor has a magnificent view out over Nuremberg – a reward for climbing the steep hill up to this point – taking in the old city, the suburbs and in the distance the mountainous area of the Franconian Alb.

It is comparatively easy to make out the extent of old Nuremberg from this vantage point. The thick, round towers in the city wall, built to guard the original four city gates, provide the required orientation. Around the year 1500, Nuremberg was home to between 40,000 and 50,000 people and was therefore one of the largest cities in the German-speaking area of Europe. Indeed, due to its favourable position on the trade routes, it appeared to many contemporaries as the centre of Europe. This is how the astronomer Johannes Regiomontanus, for example, described the city.

However, with a dry, sandy soil, lack of a navigable river, and no deposits of raw materials, it was not so much Nuremberg's location as the effects of various political developments that helped the settlement achieve greatness. Following the destruction of a castle here in the tenth century (see stopping point 2, The Imperial Castle) the city's growth benefited from the es-

RINBERGA
Vulgo
Nurmberg.

The horseshoe-shaped imperial forests that surround Nuremberg were entrusted to the city by the emperor. Their continued survival was ensured by Peter Stromer in 1368, when he devised the plantation process for coniferous forests. Painting on parchment, Erhard Etzlaub, 1516.

tablishment of the diocese of Bamberg, by Emperor Henry II, in 1007. When Henry bestowed the nearby royal court of Fürth on the diocese, this stronghold was lost to the Empire. The obvious solution was to rebuild the former castle on the 'Norenberc' hill as the new imperial fortification. This took place at the very latest during the reign of Heinrich III (1039-1056), whose stay at the castle in the summer of 1050 can be inferred from the first piece of written evidence for the existence of Nuremberg. Here, on July 14, 1050 the emperor signed the so-called Sigena Document. Its contents deal with a private legal matter: a bondswoman named Sigena was granted her freedom — possibly so she could marry a nobleman. The circumstances surrounding the document are unclear but there must have been a fortification on the hill to accommodate the

9

A view of Nuremberg from the Freiung of the imperial castle. The expanse of the medieval city is indicated by the position of the gate towers. Prominent are the two parish churches of St. Sebaldus and St. Lawrence, with their late Gothic choirs and double spires. Photo from Ferdinand Schmidt, 1890.

emperor. This was the beginning of Nuremberg's development as a city.

Starting on the southern side of the castle hill, a settlement began to form, stretching down to today's St. Sebaldus' Church. The streets and lanes followed natural contours. However, the wet pastureland near the River Pegnitz limited further expansion southwards. It was only in the 12th century that a well laid-out settlement took shape on the higher southern bank of the river, in a flood-proof area between St. Lawrence's Church and the White Tower.

A further stage in the development was reached when a wall was built round these two small 'towns'. Its course can still be traced on maps today. The Laufer Schlag Tower and the White Tower were once part of this wall and are clearly visible from the Freiung.

By the middle of the 14th century more room was required in the walled city – Nuremberg had grown into a booming trade centre. Further expansion created more living space: in particu-

et auf der Veſting die Freyung genant, in Nürnberg.
a.Kat Burg b.die St. Margaretha Kirche, c.der Hoiner Sturn.
d. die St. Walburgis Kirche.

Vüe du Château Imperial sur la Place de ſreiung à Nürnberg.
a. le Château b. l'Eglise de St. Marguerite c. la Tour du Château, d. l'Eglise
de St. Walbourg.

View of the imperial castle from the Freedom Area (Freiung): An archway leads to the outer courtyard of the castle. In the background, the Heathen's Tower (Heidenturm), and behind it the Great Hall (Palas) and women's chambers (Kemenatenbau). Coloured copper engraving by Johann Adam Delsenbach (1687-1765).

lar in the east, south and south west the city boundaries were extended. This large city of the late Middle Ages, surrounded by a wall over five kilometres long – the greater part of which has survived to this day – had reached the fullest extent of its expansion.

Looking out from the Freiung wall, the medieval city appears to have been preserved almost intact. But this appearance is deceptive. More than 90 percent of the old city was destroyed in WWII. However, because the most important historical buildings were re-erected and the reconstruction of the city retained to a large extent the former building alignments and roof landscape, the effect of the devastation is only noticeable on closer inspection.

②

The Imperial Castle

A Centre of the Empire

Emperor Ludwig the Bavarian (1314-1347) often stayed in Nuremberg and improved the city's standing by means of numerous privileges. In gratitude the town council placed a relief of the emperor in the town hall. This was partly destroyed in WWII. Minature painting in imitation of the relief, from around 1560/70.

■ An archway leads from the Freiung to the actual imperial castle. The entrance at this point is guarded by the 30-metre-high Sinwell Tower (Sinwellturm) – the name means 'round tower' in medieval German – built from sandstone ashlar. Not to be missed is the panoramic view from the top. For centuries, two towers saw service here: you always had to be on the lookout for fire or approaching danger, be it in the form of enemies or storms. The tower was also the nucleus of the castle's defence system and the last place of refuge. Indeed, the German verb "türmen", which means "to make a getaway" is derived from this defensive function of the "Turm". The original entrance was about halfway up the tower. It is now bricked up but recognisable if you look closely at the part of the tower wall facing the well house.

The well house lies at the foot of the Sinwell Tower. Since 1563 the house has protected the deep well from pollution. The well is fitted with a bucket wheel, enabling water to be raised from the bottom of the circa 50-metre-deep shaft. A visit to the house is a very special experience: with the help of lit candles and a mirror, you can appreciate the depth of the well, which was dug in the 12th century. Even at the bottom the candles

The castle complex crowns the outline of the city. On the left, the ensemble of the imperial castle comprising the Great Hall, Heathen's Tower, Sinwell Tower and Heaven's Gate (Himmelstor). On the right, the Five-cornered Tower – the remains of the counts' castle – and finally the imperial stables and the Luginsland tower. The high building covered in coats of arms and lying at the foot of the complex is a stylised version of the town hall. Minature painting from the Haller Book, 1533/36.

do not go out, indicating the high oxygen content and quality of the water. Enormous effort was expended in constructing the well. Imagine the physically demanding manual labour involved in driving a shaft into the rock down to the level of the main market and removing the waste material.

Before entering the inner courtyard of the castle, the visitor's attention is drawn to the Heathen's Tower (Heidenturm) at the western end of the outer courtyard. The famous double chapel joined to the tower is the architectural highlight of every castle tour. The upper chapel, with its slim Gothic pillars, is connected to the lower chapel by an opening in the floor. The social hierarchy of the Middle Ages is clearly visible here: the emperor's courtiers attending the church service were in the lower, the high-ranking nobles

View from the altar in the upper chapel to the imperial gallery. The four slender pillars bear the vault while the opening in the floor between them provides access to the lower chapel. The pillar to the left in the foreground is the one mentioned in the legend of the pact between the Devil and the master builder. Photo, 1935.

in the upper chapel and above them the imperial family had its own gallery. One of the four pillars in the upper chapel is held together in the middle by a ring. According to the legend, the master builder made a pact with the Devil, in order to get the chapel finished quickly. The Devil offered to bring four pillars from Rome. However, if he managed to do this before the master builder (who was also a priest) could say Mass, his soul would belong to the Devil. The priest agreed to the deal but as the Devil flew in with the fourth pillar, he ended the Mass prematurely with the words "Ite missa est". Having lost the deal, the Devil smashed the pillar to the ground and that is why it is now held together in the middle by a ring.

In the inner courtyard of the castle, with its Great Hall (Palas) and women's chambers (Kemenatenbau) building, there is no extravagance on the scale of later Renaissance or Baroque palaces. Although it looks more like a large manor, this part of the castle complex was one of the political centres of the Holy Roman Empire. When the first castle was actually built is uncertain. The most recent excavations have revealed that the first fortification was already in existence in the tenth century. It may have been a castle for nobles, possibly erected by the counts of Schweinfurt. It is certain that this first castle was destroyed – perhaps in 1003. At that time Heinrich II quelled an uprising of these counts and de-

A rainbow over the imperial castle. The picture shows the castle's outer courtyard from the east, with the Sinwell Tower (right) and the well house (centre). The imperial double-headed eagle has been painted on the closed door to the inner courtyard. To the left of the door is the Heathens' Tower. Coloured copperplate engraving, 18th century.

stroyed their castles. Later, the empire required a new fortification in this region. Thus, a new castle took shape (see the stopping point Freiung), assuming its present dimensions to a large extent in the first half of the 13th century.

Already in the late Middle Ages the castle monarchs found the accommodation at the top of the hill uncomfortable. Only the Kemenate building (women's chambers) was heatable and so they preferred to stay in the houses of the well-to-do citizens. The castle however, retained its representative functions and remained a symbol of the bond between Nuremberg, the emperor and the empire. Its unmistakeable silhouette rises like a trademark over the city and no doubt inspired the words of the local advertisement: "Protection and Security under the Sign of the Castle".

③

The Imperial Stables

A Granary and Stable for Horses

An audacious leap over the castle moat is said to have saved robber baron Eppelein von Gailingen from being executed. The supposed hoof prints are to be found in the sandstone of the cornice near the Five-cornered Tower. Postcard, around 1900.

The imperial castle is not the only building on Nuremberg's castle hill. It is joined in the east by the burgrave's castle and the Nuremberg Council buildings. The king was not always present, so he appointed a burgrave or castle count as his permanent representative. These burgraves built their own castle at the eastern and at that time only, entrance to the imperial castle and thus acted as 'gate keepers'. However, the count was also the most senior judge of the regional court, toll- and tax collector and custodian of the imperial forests. The Zollern family in particular, who had held the office since 1192, took advantage of this position of power and were thereby able to lay the foundations for the later Margravates of Ansbach and Bayreuth.

The more self-confident the citizens of Nuremberg became, the more they competed for power with the burgraves. Eventually, the castle count moved his residence to Cadolzburg near Fürth and handed his castle in Nuremberg over to a bailiff. The castle was eventually destroyed in 1420, as the result of a feud between the Zoller family and the Dukes of Bavaria. In 1427 the ruins were sold to Nuremberg City Council and

Angefangen an S. Leonhar-
di tag im 1494 Jar Vnd an S.
Leonhardi tag des 95 Jar volbracht.

Older cityscapes show a large gap between the Five-cornered Tower (left) and Luginsland (right). The plaque reproduced at the top of the drawing above informs us that the Kaiserstallung has filled this space since 1494/95. The plaque itself was placed over the entrance to the building, which today serves as a youth hostel. Watercolour, second half of the 16th century.

most of the area has remained an overgrown rubble heap. A road leads through the middle into the imperial castle. On the right and left, the Five-cornered Tower and the Walpurgis Chapel are all that remain of the burgrave's castle.

The conflict with the city council took architectural form in 1377 with the construction of a tower bearing the curious name Luginsland ("look / peep into the country"). The Nuremberg citizens allegedly augmented an older, pre-existing tower in only 40 days, so it seems they wanted not so much to look into the country as peep into the burgrave's castle! In 1494 the gap between Luginsland and the Five-cornered Tower was filled when the city architect Hans Beheim built one of his distinctive granaries here. It was designed such that horses could be kept on the ground floor – hence the name Kaiserstallung (imperial stables).

17

④

The City Fortifications

Protected by a Strong Wall

Viewed from outside the wall, the city fortifications appear impregnable. The moat and its towers were placed in front of the actual wall. Ferdinand Schmidt's photo shows the Frauentorgraben moat area between the Färber- and Sterntor gates. Photo, around 1870.

■ The Vestnertor gate leads northwards out of the castle complex. Leaving the tunnel area of the gate, visitors can stand on the bridge over the moat and view the most impressive part of the city fortifications. To keep up with the latest developments in weapons technology, Maltese master builder Antonio Fazuni constructed an impressive defence system here. Three bastions protect the city wall between the Vestnertor and Gamekeeper's Gate (Tiergärtnertor). These bulwarks served as a defence against artillery attack

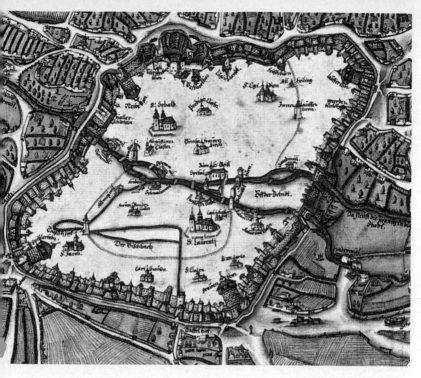

Nuremberg's wall is about five kilometres long. This map from the Pfinzing Atlas shows the four round towers at the main gates and the numerous other towers around the wall. Together, they gave the city its defensive character. The light brown line in the eastern part of the Sebaldus section of the old city and in the Lawrence settlement indicate the position and extent of the preceding wall. Coloured pen and ink drawing, 1594.

and had the added advantage that the defenders could place canons here. The zig-zag pattern made it possible to fire at the enemy from the rear, should any of them reach the wall area. To safeguard the moat, a casemate-system was constructed at the bottom of the wall. Gates invisible from the outside made it possible to conduct sorties into the moat. The Vestnertor gate indicates how well thought-out these fortifications were. The bend in the bridge made it difficult to build up enough momentum to smash in the gate at the end with a battering ram. Having followed the curve to the left to reach the gate, the enemy then had to turn sharply to the right at the tunnel entrance, spelling ultimate disaster for any battering-ram attack that had managed to get this far. In addition, through openings in the tunnel roof, the defenders could pelt intruders with pieces of wood, stones and other heavy, bulky objects.

The bastions contain a hidden jewel: the castle garden. This leads into the mayor's garden, making it possible to walk on top of the wall to the Neutor gate. Although this is the only part open to the public today, large sections of the wall survived the Second World War or were rebuilt. These impressive fortifications leave us in no doubt that Nuremberg was more than able to defend itself. Visitors who do not have the time to take a trip round the whole wall should at least make the tram journey from Plärrer to Tiergärtnertor. This stretch offers the best view of the defences and a panorama of the old city crowned by the castle.

During the period when it was an imperial city, five tower gates led into Nuremberg – Tiergärtnertor, Neutor, Spittlertor, Frauentor and Laufer Tor – and they were locked at night. The last four were rounded between 1556 and 1564, enabling them to offer more protection. Guns could be placed on the platforms and in addition, the round walls made the gates less vulnerable to artillery fire.

The strategic advantage offered by these strong fortifications was also appreciated by the great generals of the Thirty Years' War: in summer 1623 the Swedish king Gustav Adolf entrenched his army in Nuremberg. His opponent, the imperial general Wallenstein, knew that besieging the city would be a risky undertaking with an uncertain outcome. Wallenstein's solution was ingenious: instead of laying siege to Nuremberg, he built a camp for his army on the River Rednitz around Zirndorf and so rendered the city fortifications useless for Adolf. The Swedes had to engage in a pitched battle in September 1632, which went down in history as the Battle of the Old Fortress (Alte Veste). Thanks to its fortifica-

If it were possible to look though the walls of the round towers – long since a trademark of Nuremberg – a rectangular gate-tower would be visible inside. During the Second World War they were converted into bunkers and withstood the air raids. Drawing, 1970s.

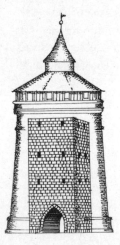

The bastions constructed by master builder Antonio Fazuni dominate the wall area between the Tiergärtnertor (right) and Vestnertor (left). They protected the imperial castle on its north flank and employed the most modern defence technology available in the 16th century. The openings of the casemates at the foot of the wall are clearly visible. Coloured pen and ink drawing, 1695.

tions, Nuremberg was never besieged or taken by force. In 1796, the French revolutionary army marched peacefully into the city.

Nuremberg was still regarded as a fortress in the Royal Bavarian Period. In the middle of the 19th century, when the growth of the suburbs forced new openings to be made in the wall, these were designed as functioning gate enclosures. However, the city lost its fortress character in 1866. The new gates, for example Max- and Marientor, were dismantled and the old Laufer Tor also disappeared. The enclosure systems can still be seen at Neutor and Spittlertor. All traffic passed through a compound (Zwinger) where it could be easily controlled. Since 1971 the former Zwinger at Frauentor has been home to the Craftsmen's Court, recreating a traditional Franconian idyll for tourists. Thus, craftmanship and gastronomy have replaced customs and traffic regulation.

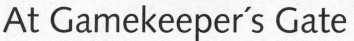

⑤

At Gamekeeper's Gate

Fire Protection and Everyday Problems

Daily life in Gamekeeper's Gate Square in the 18th century. The scene contains a number of interesting details: a coach is making its way to the gate, a man nearby is driving a pig, a beggar is receiving alms, water is being drawn from the well as a dog cocks its leg over it and children are playing with a billy goat. Copperplate engraving from Johann Adam Delsenbach (1687-1765).

■ Standing in the square at Tiergärtnertor (Gamekeeper's Gate), visitors can easily understand why old Nuremberg was called the "Treasure Chest of the German Empire" before the destruction caused by the Second World War. Half-timbered houses such as Pilatushaus on the north side or Dürer's house on the southwestern edge of the square impart a picturesque ambience. In the Romantic period, Nuremberg was renowned for its medieval and early-modern cityscape. The local tourist industry reaped the benefits, with an increasing number of visitors coming to Nuremberg from the 19th century onward – all of them seeking the German Middle Ages and the period of Dürer and Hans Sachs. The old city provided the perfect setting for the fulfilment of the tourists' expectations. Only a few adopted a more critical attitude. Hermann Hesse for instance, in his "Nuremberg Journey", is appalled by the hectic of the city. He sought and found the reason for his disappointment in himself – he should have known that Nuremberg was not an open-air museum but an industrial centre. His estimation that everything in the old city was "ready to turn to dust" appears almost prophetic today.

Prospect des Platzes bey dem Thiergärtrier Thor, in Nurmberg. Vüe de la Place auprés de la Porte dite au Parc à Nuremberg.
1. Das Thiergärtner Thor, 2. der Weg nach dem Milchmarckt, 3. der Weg in die Zißelgaßen, 4. der neue Thurn.

Barbara Dürer, the mother of the famous artist, was one of the prominent residents living at Gamekeeper's Gate. In 1509, together with her son, his wife Agnes and the complete workshop, she moved into the house on the southwestern edge of the square. Oil painting by Albrecht Dürer, around 1490.

Fortunately, some parts of the old city were saved from the firestorm of 1945. It is not difficult to recognise the present-day Gamekeeper's Gate Square in Johann Adam Delsenbach's print from the middle of the 18th century. A closer look at the work reveals something of the housing conditions in old Nuremberg. For example, the ground floors of the half-timbered houses are all made of stone. The kitchen was normally located here, so building in stone offered protection – cooking on an open fire was extremely dangerous. The fire regulations also stipulated that the houses were to be constructed with the longer side, not the gable, facing into the street. This meant that a fire in the roof area would not result in burning material falling onto the roofs of neighbouring houses. It was precisely this law that gave Nuremberg's streets and roof landscape their special character. A look down Albrecht-Dürer Street, which is next to Dürer's house and leads into the square, illustrates the fact that this char-

23

Only a few streets in the medieval city were paved, so people often protected their normal footwear with a type of overshoe. This manservant is wearing a pair while he sweeps the street with a large broom. The shoes are called "Trippen" in German. Watercolour, around 1425.

The whitewashed fire-protection wall between Dürer's House and the neighbouring building can be clearly seen in this picture. The ground floor and first floor walls are made of stone, in compliance with the fire regulations. Photo, 2008.

acter provided the architectural orientation during the rebuilding period after the war.

Wells were the main means of supplying water to the inhabitants of the medieval city. In most cases, for instance at Gamekeeper's Gate (Tiergärtnertor), they offered only groundwater. The quality of this groundwater was poor, due to the use of cesspits for waste-water disposal. As a result, the few wells that were fed by springs were very popular, for example the Beautiful Fountain (Schöner Brunnen), which obtained its water from the imperial forest area.

Only a few city streets were paved throughout. Moreover, pets and livestock frequented the lanes and this increased the amount of dirt and filth. Add to this the stench created by dungheaps, sewage ditches and pre-industrial trades and it becomes clear that the "romantic" picture of a medieval city, easily conjured up by today's visitor at places like Tiergärtnertor, is very much a product of wishful thinking projected onto the past.

The most celebrated house on the square is Albrecht Dürer's former residence. To this day, Dürer is doubtless Nüremberg's most famous son. The artist bought the building in 1509 and moved here with his wife Agnes, his mother and his entire workshop. Since 1828 the house has been a museum dedicated to Dürer's work and influence. Miraculously, it survived the air raids of

the Second World War. Its rapid renovation and re-opening in 1949 carried an important message: even though the unique ensemble of the old city has been destroyed forever, the most important public buildings should be restored so that Nuremberg remains a popular tourist destination.

The "Brown Hare" illustrates
Dürer's love of natural motifs.
Watercolour, 1503.

⑥

The Albrecht Dürer Monument

Nuremberg's Most Famous Son

Albrecht Dürer's famous self-portrait: clad in his fur coat, the self-confident, Christlike artist stares at the observer. The face of the statue that forms part of the Dürer monument was modelled on this painting. Oil painting on wood, 1500.

■ At the milk market, where milk and cheese used to be sold, Albrecht Dürer stands self-confidently on the plinth of his monument, holding some painting utensils in his hand. Born in the city in 1471, he remains to this day Nuremberg's most famous citizen. Dürer's mother was also born in Nuremberg. His father, on the other hand, was an immigrant Hungarian goldsmith. Albrecht was apprenticed to Michael Wolgemut, who ran a successful painting workshop at the foot of the castle. Dürer's copperplate engravings, woodcuts, altars, portraits and stained-glass windows made his name famous far beyond the walls of Nuremberg and helped him amass a sizeable fortune. This wealth enabled him to buy the house at Tiergärtnertor in 1509, which served as living quarters and workshop. Dürer's importance lies in the many innovations, inspired by Italy, that he brought to German art. For instance, his water-colour of a hare, one of his most reproduced works, takes up a motif that had been largely ignored before Dürer's time – nature itself.

After his death in 1528, collectors caused Dürer's works to be scattered throughout the world. Only a small selection has remained in Nuremberg and this can be viewed in the city's German National Museum. Another look at the

Admirers gaze up at the statue of Albrecht Dürer. Cast in the Burgschmiet foundry, this part of the monument is a consequence of the Dürer celebrations in 1828, that marked the 300th anniversary of the artist's death. Coloured steel-engraving.

monument, this time from behind, reveals patches and a tear in Dürer's gown. These supposedly refer to Agnes's meanness and her neglect of Dürer. She was rumoured to be a nagging wife. Even though it has no verifiable basis, this negative picture of Agnes was fostered for centuries. In any case, Dürer's wife has been honoured in Nuremberg – within sight of his monument a street (Agnesgasse) has been named after her.

27

⑦

The Tawers' Street

Stinking Hides and Rich People

The picturesque ensemble of half-timbered houses at the western end of Weißgerbergasse gives an indication of what large sections of Nuremberg's old city looked like before the destruction wrought by the Second World War. Photo, 2008.

The Tawers' Street (Weißgerbergasse) is one of the best-preserved streets in the old city. It is a picturesque ensemble of 22 craftmen's houses, most of them half-timbered buildings. Closed to normal traffic, the street is ideal for those wishing to linger for a while. However, at the time the tanners lived here, the atmosphere was far from idyllic. The tawers were tanners who produced fine leather from calf-, sheep- and goatskin. This was then used to make gloves or clothes. The coarser leather from cow- or pig hide was made by the "Lederer" tanners. Tanning hides required large amounts of water, so it was very important that the industry was near the Pegnitz. The smell that resulted from the process was so intense that the saying "Stinking hides make people rich" established itself in the vernacular.

There were many different types of Nuremberg tradesmen. As well as those associated with the basic trades i.e. bakers, butchers, brewers,

Der hern bruder der do stund
hieß peter lederer

Leather was much in demand, not just for clothing and shoes but also for book covers, saddles and the small parts of animal harnesses, weapons and other devices. The picture shows a tanner soaking the animal skin in a wooden tub. Behind him is a hide that has been stretched out to dry. Watercolour from around 1425.

blacksmiths, tanners, cobblers, etc., there were more specialised subdivisions. In particular, the metal-workers attained international distinction. Knives, funnels, bowls and candle holders made from metal – whether it be iron or brass – together with every kind of weapon, were among the main exports. In armoury and weapons production, the suits of armour made by the platers were highly regarded, as were Nuremberg swords, crossbows, guns and artillery. The smiths also achieved considerable success. In particular, astronomical devices produced by the compass

Der hymen brudee dee do starb
hieß Dyetrich Oschorkenzeher

An invention from 1415 was guarded in Nuremberg like a state secret: the mechanical process of wire-drawing with the aid of water power. However, in the picture manual labour is still being used: the wire-drawer uses the momentum of a swing to pull the wire more easily through the drawplate. Wire was an important element in weapons production e.g. for chain mail. Watercolour from around 1425.

makers enjoyed a good reputation, as did musical instruments manufactured in the city.

The more prosperous the city became the more the work of the gold- and silversmiths came to the fore, reaching its peak with Wenzel Jamitzer (1507/08-1585). The letterpress printing method also found its way into the city at an early date. The publisher and businessman Anton Koberger (1440/45-1513) created one of the first printing empires in Germany. His presses produced world-famous books such as "Schedel's World Chronicle" (Schedelsche Weltchronik).

Although Nuremberg's success in the Middle Ages owed much to these tradesmen, they were excluded from influential participation in the city's political life. Since the craftmen's revolt of 1347/48, self-governing guilds had ceased to exist. As a concessionary measure following the uprising, eight representatives were given seats on the Inner Council (Innerer Rat) but without voting rights. Thus, while the craftsmen's reputation had been recognised, their influence remained negligible.

High-quality products from Nuremberg's craftsmen can be admired today in the German National Museum. On the right, the "Schlüsselfeld Ship", a centrepiece from a Nuremberg goldsmith's workshop around 1500. The city's platers produced armour (below, right) and the compass makers manufactured high-quality measuring instruments such as the astrolabe (below, left). Photos, from around 1990.

31

⑧

The Church of St. Sebaldus

Nuremberg's Patron Saint and His Church

According to the legend, Sebaldus' corpse was laid on an oxcart and the place where the oxen finally refused to go any further became the burial site. The present-day church was built over his grave. Section of a tapestry, from around 1410.

■ Viewed from the north, the Church of St. Sebaldus is particularly impressive: the mighty east choir, the nave with its Romanesque window arches, the Gothic aisle and the two towers blend harmoniously together and bear witness to the building's long history. This is the oldest parish church in Nuremberg and was erected on the site of an earlier chapel dedicated to the apostle Peter. Sebaldus, the church's present-day patron saint, might not be familiar even to those well-acquainted with the calendar of saints. Nevertheless, he remains a major personality in the history of Nuremberg.

Sebaldus was a hermit who probably lived in the nearby forests in the 11th century. Already regarded as a saintly man in his own lifetime, people started to go on pilgrimages to his grave very soon after his death. In the second written reference to Nuremberg – found in the annals of Niederaltaich Monastery – there is mention of pilgrims making their way to Sebaldus' grave in 1070. These travellers were by no means unimportant for the growth of the young settlement. The saint's grave was initially located in the chapel built prior

View of the nave and side aisles. The swallow's nest (Schwalbennest) Organ (1440) can be seen behind the pillar. It was destroyed in the Second World War. Watercolour pen and ink drawing from Georg Christoph Wilder, 1831.

to today's church. However, the present-day building provides an appropriate and dignified setting for his final resting place. Placed under the arches of the Gothic choir, the tomb – redesigned between 1508 and 1519 by the workshop of brass-founder Peter Fischer – is the church's greatest art treasure. Inside the tomb a chest covered in silver plate contains the relics – the bones actually do come from a man who lived around the year 1000.

The impressive collection of pictures and figures that decorate the tomb are rich in detail and relate Christianity's victory over the pagan world of antiquity. Consequently the Christ Child, as Lord of the Worlds, has been placed on the highest part of the tomb, the top of the central tower. In contrast, the lower part is occupied by putti and figures from antique mythology. The inner surfaces here are covered with reliefs based on events from the Sebaldus legend e.g. the "miracle of the icicles", when the saint allegedly used icicles to make a fire. Around the actual shrine are statues of the twelve apostles. Thus Sebaldus, as the city's patron saint, occupies the same level as the first followers of Jesus. Above them, the twelve Old Testament prophets represent the Jewish roots of Christianity. On the narrow sides of the lower section of the tomb two figures stand out: Sebaldus and the artist Peter Vischer, who self-confidently presents himself in his working clothes. The animals at the very bottom are also symbols. The dolphins at the four corners represent Christ. The snails, bearing the full weight of the tomb, stand for the Resurrection – like the snail, that disappears into its shell to reappear again, Christ was taken down from the cross, laid in the tomb and rose again from the dead.

Statuette of Peter Vischer from the tomb of St. Sebaldus. The tomb created by Fischer and his sons is a unique combination of Gothic and Renaissance: the main structure and the arches above the shrine are Gothic in form, while the figures in the lower part stem are Renaissance style. Photo, 2007.

The tomb of Sebaldus and the many other works of art make it easy to forget that this is a Protestant church. Nuremberg was one of the early supporters of Martin Luther, deciding in 1525 to adopt the changes demanded by the Reformation movement. The Bishop of Bamberg's authority was no longer recognised and the city council made the decisions regarding ecclesiastical matters. However, the Nuremberg Reformers,

A painting commissioned by Lorenz Tucher (†1503) decorates the north wall of the choir. This section shows the left side of the work. St. Lawrence, the patron saint of the dead man kneeling down in the middle, presents him to St. Peter so he can enter paradise. Oil painting, 1513.

Over time, the legend of Sebaldus was increasingly embellished. In this sculpture from around 1400 he appears in noble dress. The staff and shells identify him as a pilgrim. Photo, 2007.

led by the preacher Andreas Osiander and the town clerk Lazarus Spengler, were moderate: no works of art were removed from churches and there was no violent closure of the monasteries. Thus, valuable church art from the late Middle Ages had a better chance of survival in those regions that came under Nuremberg's sphere of influence.

In the Second World War the church was badly damaged – picture boards on the nave pillars document this. However, beginning in 1940, the works of art had been removed from the churches and placed in the art bunker (Kunstbunker), so the originals could be brought back after rebuilding. In this way, the churches retained something of the atmosphere of the late Middle Ages. The tomb of Sebaldus remained in the choir. Covered by a protective wall, it survived the bombing.

⑨

The Town Hall

Centre of Power

Placed above the main entrance, the pelican feeding its chicks with its own blood symbolises the town council's readiness to sacrifice itself for its subjects. The letters PLEG stand for "Prudentia, legibus et gratia" – "We rule with prudence, justice and mercy". Photo, 2008.

■ Opposite the east choir of St.Sebaldus Church, the long façade of the town hall exhibits Renaissance splendour. Jakob Wolff the Elder and his son Jakob Wolff the Younger began construction of the façade in 1616 and this is why the town hall is often referred to as the "Wolff Building". Unfortunately, with the onset of the Thirty Years' War in 1618, the original plan, which envisaged a larger building, was never realised. However, the town hall that the Wolffs did actually complete is impressive enough. Resembling an aristocratic city-palace, it appears to fulfil its representative function more successfully than the medieval imperial castle.

Nuremberg's council had practised this type of civic self-portrayal for some time. The Great Hall, located behind the southern section of the town hall façade, was built between 1332 and 1340. At the time, it was regarded as the largest secular room in use north of the Alps. Outside, its Gothic windows can be seen by walking towards the rear of the town hall at the southern end.

Inside, the visitor can still get a sense of the Great Hall's original splendour, despite the fact that the wall paintings by Albrecht Dürer were irretrievably destroyed during World War II. The reliefs on the east wall of the interior still bear wit-

A view towards the western end of the Great Hall. The 39-metre-long room was the meeting place for the municipal court and the emperor also received the citizens' tribute here. Important events such as the Religious Disputation (Religionsgespräch) of 1525 and the Peace Banquet (Friedensmahl) in 1649 found their appropriate setting in the hall. Oil painting on wood, by Lorenz Hess, 1626.

ness to the destruction. They depict Emperor Ludwig the Bavarian and the female figures "Norimberga and Brabantia", these last two symbolising the conferral of trade privileges. The imperial throne was also positioned on the east wall. Thus, the council members never lost sight of their close alliance with the emperor, a relationship which guaranteed Nuremberg's independence. The throne can be admired today in the city's Fembohaus Museum.

Day-to-day politics did not take place in the Great Hall. Instead, the councillors met in the adjoining "Ratsstube", a smaller council chamber.

Town Hall

37

The council, which governed the city-state of Nuremberg, came into existence in the Middle Ages. Its members were recruited from merchant families who had become rich through trade. In other imperial cities, the craftsmen possessed considerable influence, but in Nuremberg they were granted just eight seats on the council and these representatives had only an advisory function. The caste of governing merchant families increasingly formed themselves into an exclusive social class. They cultivated an aristocratic lifestyle and, as the centuries passed, gave up their trading houses. In 1696/97 Emperor Leopold I ennobled all the patrician families of Nuremberg. The imperial city was ruled by a strict oligarchy: until 1806 the patrician families held the reins of power and none of the other inhabitants had any direct influence on Nuremberg politics.

The council's conviction that it provided the best form of government finds symbolic expression above the middle portal of the town hall: the two reclining female figures are "Justitia" and "Prudentia" i.e. Justice and Prudence. Justice is equipped with the weighing scales of balance and Prudence with the mirror of self-knowledge. A small group of figures in a central position above them complete the scene: a pelican pierces its breast to feed the hungry chicks with its own blood. This symbol of self-sacrifice was often used

The patrician families of Nuremberg came originally from the royal bondservants and the merchant class. Many also moved from other cities to the up-and-coming metropolis. With the Dance Statute (Tanzstatut) of 1521, these families distanced themselves from the lower classes. They increasingly embraced an aristocratic lifestyle, evidenced by their coats of arms, castle-like manors and the lordship they exercised over numerous peasants in the surrounding area.

Volckamer
v. Kirchensittenbach.

Freiherren v. Imhoff.

Freiherren
Kreß v. Kreßenstein.

A member of the highest council committee – a triumvirate of two treasurers (Losunger) and the third, high official (Oberer Hauptmann) – bears symbolically the burden of responsibility for Nuremberg. The patrician government firmly established itself after the craftsmen's revolt of 1348/49 and functioned almost unchanged up until the end of the city's independence in 1806. Detail of a watercolour pen and ink drawing from around 1580.

in Christian iconography to represent Christ's death on the cross.

The town council was also empowered to administer justice, including the death penalty. This authority, essential to the council's self-image, explains why there is a dungeon two floors beneath the council hall, where those awaiting trial were detained. Prisoners were also tortured here. The council was always kept informed of the pre-trial investigations.

Freiherren Löffelholz v. Colberg.

Freiherren Tucher von Simmelsdorf.

Freiherren Welser v. Neunhof.

⑩

Weighing House
The Heart of Nuremberg Trade

The armed men accompanying the convoy of merchants indicate how dangerous trade could be – rich pickings for thieves and robber barons. Provision of an armed escort for travellers and businessmen was one of the most important imperial privileges bestowed on the city. Photo, 1980s.

▌The two weighing houses in the city were at the heart of Nuremberg's trade. The older house was located in the street called Waaggasse near the main market square. Built in 1497/98 by Hans Beheim, it does not exist anymore. However, its scale balance is featured in a relief by Adam Kraft on the Chamber of Trade and Industry building.

All incoming and outgoing goods passed through the weighing house, so that the municipal master weigher could determine the amount of duty to be paid. The weighed goods were then stamped and sealed. This ensured that those items of merchandise intended for export were quality products from Nuremberg.

A functioning system of trade was essential for the growth of the city. From early on, Nuremberg's citizens endeavoured to secure trade privileges. The city's location in the centre of Europe, enabled it to establish commercial links in all directions: to Flanders and Brabant, France, Northern Italy, Austria, Bohemia and Poland. By around 1500, Nuremberg had a monopoly in some trades e.g. in spices. No wonder the Nuremberg merchants were called "Pfeffersäcke" in German, lit. "pepper sacks". The German word means "moneybags".

However, a dramatic change in Nuremberg's status followed the discovery of America in 1492. Sea trade became more and more important and as a result Nuremberg was increasingly marginalized.

An impressive wall painting from 1910, on the side of the Chamber of Trade and Commerce building facing the main market square, depicts a convoy of merchants. The motto underneath reads "Nuremberg's goods are legion in every region".

Adam Kraft created the ideal snapshot of a master weigher going about his everyday business. He stands under a huge beam-balance and observes the pointer on the beam. To his right a servant places weights on one scale, to weigh the goods in the scale to his left. A merchant can be seen sullenly reaching into his money bag to pay the duty. Photo, 1980s.

⑪

Main Market Square

Nuremberg's Parlour

Already in the 16th century, stalls selling food dominated the main market. The western zone (left) was known as the "Herrenmarkt". The German word refers to the stock exchange which opened here in 1560. Oil painting by Lorenz Strauch, 1594.

■ This square is the centre of Nuremberg's old city. It still serves mainly as a marketplace for the sale of fruit, vegetables and other fresh food. However, on certain fixed dates in the calendar, for instance during the Christmas Market or the "Crockery Market" (Häfelesmarkt) at Easter and in the autumn, its stalls are moved to the Museum Bridge and Lorenz Square. At such times the Market Square belongs exclusively to the sellers of Christmas decorations, gingerbread cake

The murder of Nuremberg Jews and the destruction of their houses and synagogue preceded the construction of the main market that began in 1350. Wood carving from Schedel's World Chronicle, 1494.

(Lebkuchen) and mulled wine or porcelain, kitchen utensils and aprons.

The crowds that gather between the red and white tarpaulins of the market stalls are particularly large at 12 midday. People gaze up at the clock on the west façade of Our Lady's Church (Frauenkirche) and wait for the "little men walking" ("Männleinlaufen") performance. The clock dates from 1509 and recalls the "Golden Bull". Issued in Nuremberg by Emperor Charles IV in

43

1356, this was one of the constitutional laws of the Holy Roman Empire of the German Nation and regulated the election of the emperor. The figures, somewhat disrespectfully named "little men" (Männlein), are none other than the seven electors, who appear in order to pay their respects to the enthroned emperor.

The main market square dates from the reign of Charles IV. Unfortunately, the history of this part of the city reveals that the construction of the market provided a pretext for murder. Since 1349 this area in the middle of the city had been part of the Jewish quarter of Nuremberg. The synagogue stood on the site now occupied by Our Lady's Church. In the early evening of the Feast of St. Nicholas, on 5th December 1348, Nuremberg citizens stormed and ravaged the Jewish houses, killing 582 people in the process. This was the second murderous pogrom against the Nuremberg Jews in the space of 50 years. Already in 1298 unrest in Franconia had led to more than 600 people being murdered in Nuremberg because they belonged to the Jewish community. The explanatory context for the 1348 pogrom is provided by the failed craftmen's revolt a few months before. The old patricians had re-established their hold on the council, following a period of confusion after the death of Emperor Ludwig the Bavarian – in which the city had been ruled by a party sympathetic to the craftsmen. As a consequence, huge sums were owed to the Jewish money-lenders. Thus, one reason for the pogrom was that it provided people with an opportunity to avoid paying their debts.

Those who took action against the Jews even obtained a degree of imperial support: the emperor issued a document giving permission for the

This sculpture of a "Jews' sow" ("Judensau"), on the east choir of St. Sebaldus' Church, pointed in the direction of the Jewish quarter. The oppressive, anti-Semitic representation depicts Jews sucking at the teats of a sow. Jews regarded the animal as unclean. Photo, 2007.

The arrival of the imperial regalia (crown jewels), as seen through the eyes of 19th century Romanticism. Hidden under a cargo of fish, the regalia of the Holy Roman Empire were brought to Nuremberg by order of Emperor Sigismund in 1424. The public exhibition of the regalia and various sacred relics (Heiltumsweisung) took place at the market square once a year. Oil painting by Paul Ritter, 1883.

construction of the main- and fruit market and the building of a church dedicated to St. Mary. What the document did not make clear was that this required the expropriation of the Jews, which then took place in such a cruel fashion. A commemorative plaque on the north side of Our Lady's Church, a Star of David in the floor of the east choir and the design of the church's tabernacle remind us of the market area's Jewish past. The tabernacle design, which dates from 1987, resembles the Torah shrine of a synagogue, recalling the medieval building that preceded the church.

Before the Jews settled there at the end of the 12th century, the present-day market area was

The Beautiful Well is a popular motif with photographers. Today's structure, made of resistant shell-limestone, was placed here in the 19th century because by this time the original sandstone figures had become very weather-beaten. In the background to the left, the so-called Eisenbach House. Watercolour drawing, 19th century.

undeveloped, as this was a high water zone of the Pegnitz. The Jews had to stabilize their houses by means of wooden stakes driven into the wet subsoil. When the houses were demolished, a central market square arose – something that had been missing from medieval Nuremberg. The "Beautiful Well" (Schöne Brunnen) was erected on the northwest corner of the square in 1378. Decorated with figures, its Gothic structure is in effect a synopsis of the medieval world-view: biblical figures, saints, heroes and the personification of the "seven liberal arts" i.e. the subjects taught at the medieval universities. Fed by its own water pipe, the well provided the Nuremberg in-

The Christmas Market ("Kindleinsmarkt") made its first appearance around 1600. Here, presents for children could be bought in the period leading up to Christmas. It returned to the main market square in 1933, having moved in the intervening period to various locations e.g. Schütt Island and Prinzregentenufer. The Christmas Market attracts millions of visitors every year and is one of the oldest German markets of its kind. Photo, 2005.

habitants with fresh drinking water from outside the city. The widespread belief that the well was intended as a spire for Our Lady's Church is nothing more than an attractive fiction.

Sometimes another legend causes people to queue at the well. The "golden" ring in the southwest side of the elaborate latticework supposedly bears witness to an unhappy love affair. An apprentice locksmith fell in love with his master's daughter. However, the master did not think very highly of the apprentice, called him a good-for-nothing and ordered him to leave the household. The night he left Nuremberg, he inserted a brass ring in the well latticework to show his skill as a craftsman. The ring could be rotated and was so artfully worked that it appeared seamless. Today numerous visitors to Nuremberg turn the ring – it is supposed to make their wishes come true.

⑫

At the Executioner's House

Leprosy, Butchers' Benches and the Executioner

The ensemble of Executioner's House and Executioner's Tower before the destruction of the southern part of the building in 1595: the adventurous wooden structure of the old Executioner's Bridge between the tower and Tallow House (Unschlitthaus) is easily discernable. When broken ice caused it to collapse in 1595, several people lost their lives. Coloured drawing by Lorenz Strauch, 1579.

■ One of the most-photographed ensembles in Nuremberg is located on the western tip of the Trödelmarktinsel (Flea Market Island): Executioner's Bridge, Executioner's House and the Wine Barn. The executioner's tower on the island, the house itself and the water tower on the north bank of the river are remains of the penultimate city wall that spanned the Pegnitz before the expansion of the city in the 14th century. To connect the Sebaldus and Lorenz sides of Nuremberg, the medieval architects choose the Trödelmarktinsel area because it was easier to erect an arched bridge over the river at this point. Later, when the completion of the new outer wall rendered the inner wall superfluous as a fortification, these river crossings, built at great expense, remained. The battlements were used as residences for city officials.

Executioner's House, spanning the northern arm of the Pegnitz, is the sole surviving river-crossing of the old wall. The dwelling of the executioner's assistant adjoined it to the south but this was pulled down after being badly damaged by broken ice and a flood in 1595. The wooden Executioner's Bridge (Henkersteg) now occupies the site.

For centuries, the tower and house formed the official residence of the Nachrichter or "after-

Executing a man by the sword in Nuremberg. The executioner reaches back with his sword as far as possible, to try to cut off the head with one stroke. Coloured pen and ink drawing from around 1600.

judge", the Nuremberg term for an executioner. The expression alludes to his function in the community – after the judge had passed sentence, he carried out the punishment, be it public humiliation, corporal punishment or the death penalty. Nuremberg's most famous Nachrichter, Franz Schmidt, lived here for about 40 years and was official executioner from 1577 to 1617. He left to posterity a diary in which he described in detail his 361 executions and 345 acts of corporal punishment. It gives a unique insight into the history of crime in Nuremberg around 1600. In 2007 a museum was opened in Executioner's House. It provides information about the history of law in Nuremberg, the office of executioner and Franz Schmidt.

It is worth exploring the tranquil area surrounding Executioner's House. The

PEGNITZ

Until 1580 women were executed by drowning them in the Pegnitz. This practice was later abolished and women were thereafter beheaded or hanged. The picture shows the first execution of women – members of a band of thieves – by hanging in Nuremberg, in February 1584. The executions were carried out at the so-called Rabenstein between Frauentor and the Galgenhof area, outside the city walls to the southeast. Coloured drawing from around 1600.

scene here in the Middle Ages was very different. Mills made use of the river to drive their water wheels, giving the Pegnitz an early-industrial character. Waste was often thrown into the river from the butchers' benches and this caused the millers to complain about the intestines that frequently ended up wrapped around their water wheels. The smell of the boiling tallow in Tallow House (Unschlitthaus) was all-pervasive.

The Wine Barn is located on the northern bank of the Pegnitz. Built between 1446 and 1448, it was first used as a "Sondersiechenhaus", an asylum for lepers. Normally they lived outside the city in one of the leper houses (Siechköbel). However, once a year, during Holy Week, they were allowed to enter the city and beg for alms. During this time, they stayed at the asylum. In 1575, when people were no longer allowed to beg for alms inside the city, the council decided to use the building as a wine barn, hence its present name.

The Pegnitz leaves the city to the west of the Max Bridge (Maxbrücke). Impressive large towers, imposing walls and a portcullis protect this potentially vulnerable area of the city fortifications. Just in front of the wall, the chain bridge (Kettensteg) spans the river. It was built in 1825 and was the first suspension bridge on the continent to be made entirely of metal. To the

south, between Kettensteg and Maxbrücke, lies one of the most modern residential areas in the old part of Nuremberg, the Kreuzgassenviertel. In WWII most of the old buildings here were totally destroyed. Construction of the new residential quarter was not completed until the 1980s.

The light of the full moon on a winter's night shines down on Executioner's House and the Wine Barn. The Pegnitz is completely frozen, offering children the chance to play on the ice. In the "little ice age" between the 16th and 19th centuries this was not unusual. Coloured print, 19th century.

Unschlitthaus and Unschlittplatz (Unschlitt Square) form an ensemble that gives the visitor a good impression of what old Nuremberg looked like before it was largely destroyed in the Second World War. When Nuremberg was an imperial city, the Tallow Office was located in Unschlitthaus and was responsible for disposing of the waste produced by the butchers. Their slaughterhouses were located on the banks of the Pegnitz between Meat Bridge (Fleischbrücke) and Executioners Bridge – hence the street name "Between the Meat Benches" ("Zwischen den Fleischbänken"). Unschlitthaus was also a granary, a precaution against famine. Today the headquarters of the Nuremberg Loan Office is located here. The institution's beginnings take us back to Nuremberg's imperial past. In 1618 the office was opened to provide credit. This imperial privilege had already been granted to the city following the expulsion of the last medieval Jewish community from Nuremberg in 1499.

⑬

Hospital of the Holy Spirit

Help for the Poor and the Sick

View of the Museum Bridge and the Hospital of the Holy Spirit. Coloured copper-engraving by Johann Adam Delsenbach (1687-1765).

The grave of Konrad Groß lies under the arcades in the Courtyard of the Crucifixion. Mourning figures surround the recumbent statue of the donator. Photo, 1980s.

■ Commerce usually dictates proceedings on the Museum Bridge (Museumsbrücke). Connecting the pedestrian zone with the main market, it is normally covered with stalls. However, looking to the west, over the parapet wall, the observer is rewarded with a view of the river at the Meat Bridge (Fleischbrücke).This is the narrowest part of the Pegnitz within the city walls. To the east is one of the most unusual "bridges" – it is actually part of the Hospital of the Holy Spirit (Heilig-Geist-Spital). Building a section of the hospital over the river was one of the great architectural feats of the municipal master-builder Hans Beheim the Elder. Born in the middle of the 15th century, this stonemason and architect made a lasting impression on the imperial city of Nuremberg. In addition to the hospital he built the imperial stables, the Toll Building (Mauthalle) and Unschlitthaus. When Beheim renovated and extended the hospital between 1506 and 1525 it could look back on a history of almost 200 years.

The hospital was founded by the merchant and patrician Konrad Groß, whose family had become rich through for-

The hospital's coat of arms combines the coat of arms of the city (right), the virgin or "harpy" eagle (left) and the dove symbolising the Holy Spirit. Coloured pen and ink drawing, 1565.

eign trade and shrewd financial transactions. Groß helped to finance the policies of Emperor Ludwig the Bavarian, so he was himself involved in imperial politics. Although this was a source of additional income for him, it also caused problems for Groß. For most of the time the emperor was in conflict with the pope and this lead to the excommunication of the emperor and his supporters. For the devout Konrad Groß the question was whether this would have any effect on his salvation of his soul. As a precautionary measure, he founded numerous religious charities. The largest of these was the Hospital of the Holy Spirit. From the point of view of the capital involved, this was one of the most substantial foundations of the European Middle Ages.

The Hospital of the Holy Spirit could not, and did not want to be, a hospital in the modern sense. It was more an institution that looked after those whom the city could not cope with in any other way: sick and lonely old people, single mothers, the disabled, the chronically ill, etc.

A nurse at work. The rule book (Leitbuch) of the Hospital of the Holy Spirit makes explicit the religious background of the foundation: the sick person is wearing a halo and is depicted as Christ himself. To care for the sick was to emulate Jesus. Minature painting on gold, from around 1400.

Those suffering from diseases known to be contagious – lepers for instance – were not accommodated in the city but in special leper houses on the arterial roads. Beheim's design for the bridge section of the hospital building i.e. the part spanning the Pegnitz, also provided a simple solution to the sewage problem: waste could be directed straight into the river.

In the middle of this building complex lies the Courtyard of the Crucifixion (Kreuzigungshof). It is worth taking a little detour to visit this part of the Spital complex. The simplest way in is through the gateway opposite Debtors' Tower (Schuldturm), between Heu- and Spitalbrücke. This atmospheric courtyard, closed on all four sides, is undoubtedly one of the most beautiful places in Nuremberg. Here the visitor stands directly above the Pegnitz – the river can be seen through the drains in the middle of the floor. The name of the courtyard dates from the 20th century, when the crucifixion group by Adam Kraft was brought to the north side of the courtyard. It belongs to a larger work – a group of Calvary figures – at the entrance to St. John's Cemetery (Johannisfriedhof).

There was space for almost a hundred sick people in the dormitory of the hospital. Coloured pan and ink drawing from around 1780.

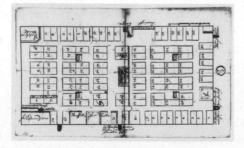

Prospect dreyer steinerner Brücken zu Nürnberg über den Pegnitz Fluß gebauet

View over the Hay Bridge (Heubrücke) looking to the west. The 1.2 kilometres of the Pegnitz within the walls of the old city is the stretch of river In Europe with the most bridges: no less than 16 bridges and buildings span the Pegnitz or one of its branches.
Coloured copper engraving by J.M. Burucker, 18th century.

At the northeast corner of the courtyard is the entrance to the Spital Church (Spitalkirche). In 1424, when Emperor Sigismund entrusted the imperial regalia to the citizens of Nuremberg "for all time", they were placed in the Spital Church, the only place of worship in Nuremberg directly under the control of the city council. During the turmoil of the Hussite Wars the regalia made the hazardous journey from Bohemia to Nuremberg. From 1424 onwards Nuremberg was responsible for ensuring that the regalia were brought to Frankfurt am Main every time a new emperor was crowned there. It was only with the approach of the French Revolutionary Army in 1796 that the last ruler of the Holy Roman Empire of the German Nation, Franz II, had the regalia moved to Vienna. They can be viewed there today in the Schatzkammer Treasury of the Hofburg Palace – the intermezzo under the National Socialists, from the annexation of Austria until the end of the war, during which time the regalia were back in Nuremberg, was very short.

(14)

ART

The Church of St. Lawrence

More than the Annunciation and the Tabernacle

Lawrence, the church's patron saint, is depicted holding a gridiron. Legend has it that, during the time of the persecution of the Christians under Emperor Valerian in 258, he was martyred by being roasted alive. Photo, 2008.

Like the northern half of the old city, the area south of the Pegnitz is also named after its main parish church: the Lawrence district. In the 12th century, the region between the Church of St. Lawrence (Lorenzkirche) and St. James' Square (Jakobsplatz), formed the nucleus of this settlement area in the fledgling city. There is clear evidence of systematic street-planning here. In the Sebaldus settlement, between the castle and the main market, the lanes and building alignments sprang up haphazardly and followed natural contours. In contrast, the streets between St. Lawrence Square and Jakobsplatz form an oval and evince medieval city-planning.

The two halves of Nuremberg on either side of the Pegnitz were joined together in the 1320s, when both were enclosed within the same city wall. Ever since, the river has divided the city into two almost equal halves. However, the area enclosed by the wall soon became too small for the the city's growing population and so work began on a new wall in the 14th century. This was completed in 1452. The Lawrence district grew markedly as a result of this expansion.

St. Lawrence's Church forms the centre of the district. The best way to approach the building is

The west façade of the Church of St. Lawrence dates from the reign of Emperor Charles IV in the middle of the 14th century. The main portal, with its rich adornment of figures and the great rose window, stands firmly in the tradition of the Gothic architecture characteristic of French cathedrals. Photo, 2008.

from the west, via the street called Karolinenstraße. This affords a good view of the impressive west façade, the two towers and the large rose window above the main portal. It pays to look closely at the wealth of decorative figures around the portal – the whole of salvific history is portrayed here, from Adam and Eve to the Last Judgement. However, it is also rewarding to look to the north from St. Lawrence's Square (Lorenzer Platz) to enjoy one of the best views of the castle. Above the Well of Virtues (Tugendbrunnen), the towers of the town hall and the Church of St. Sebaldus, the castle silhouette crowns the hill.

The two most famous works of art in the choir of St. Lawrence's Church are just a few feet away from each other: the Annunciation by Veit Stoß, framed by a wreath of gold-plated roses, and Adam Kraft's tabernacle. One of the three figures bearing the tabernacle is believed to be a self-portrait of Kraft. Photos, 2008 (left and bottom right); oil painting by Paul Ritter, 1897 (above right).

Today the visitor enters the Church of St. Lawrence via a small portal on the south side of the building. The interior appears quite uniform, due to the fact that it was built within the relatively short space of about 100 years. The construction of the west façade was completed in 1353. The choir, built in the 15th century between 1439 and 1477, integrates well with the rest of the church. It is here that the visitor can enjoy the two works of art for which the building is world-famous: the Annunciation (Engelsgruß) by Veit Stoß and the tabernacle (Sakramentshaus) by Adam Kraft.

The Annunciation, which dominates the choir, dates from 1517 and was a donation from councillor Anton Tucher. Made of lime wood, the work depicts the Archangel Gabriel greeting Mary, an incident related in the Gospel of Luke. Mary is surprised by the angel's announcement, that she of all people is to give birth to the Messiah. Veit Stoß has captured the moment brilliantly. The archangel appears as the self-confident bearer of an important message, while Mary draws back slightly in astonishment. A book she has just been reading slips from her left hand, and she brings her raised right hand towards her body in a gesture of surprise. For centuries the masterpiece was covered by a sack. This was the city's practical solution – after becoming Protestant in 1525 – to the problem of how to deal with a work of art expressing a more Catholic form of devotion.

The tabernacle is just a few steps away from the Annunciation, leaning on a northern pillar of the choir. Just as Veit Stoß knew how to carve lime

wood so that it would speak to us of the Annunciation, his contemporary, the sculptor Adam Kraft, had mastered the art of creating a breathtaking tower out of stone. The tabernacle, whose tower soars up into the vaulting, was completed in 1496. Designed for the reservation of the eucharistic bread, it was a donation from the patrician Hans Imhoff. The words "Ecce panis angelorum" – "Behold the bread of the angels" on the lattice remind us of what was kept there. However, Kraft did not create just a simple receptacle. In true Gothic manner, his work of art reaches up to heaven, each new section crowning the preceding one, so that from below it is difficult to make out clearly all the abundant figures and scenes. Beginning at the tabernacle doors, the figures relate the Passion of Jesus, from the Last Supper through to the Crucifixion and ending with the Resurrection on Easter Sunday. The whole structure is decorated with Gothic tracery. Sculptures also adorn the base of the tabernacle: three men symbolise the three stages in life – youth, the prime of life and old age. The figure in the middle, in the prime of life, is believed to be a self-portrait of Adam Kraft.

Numerous other works of art from Nuremberg's cultural heyday around 1500 can be viewed in the church. A visit to the loft area is also worthwhile. The original hoist, to which the Annunciation was attached, can still be seen there.

⑮

The Toll Building

Precaution against Famine

View inside the large storage rooms on the first floor of the Toll House. Photo by Ferdinand Schmidt, 1897.

As part of the alterations carried out in 1897/98, shops were built on the ground floor and windows put in on the first and second floors. As a result, the Toll House lost its austere appearance – formerly its gable tracery had provided the only ornamentation. Photo, after 1898.

■ The Huge Toll Building (Mauthalle), at the crossroads of Königstraße (King Street) and Hallplatz, indicates the course taken by the city wall before the expansion of Nuremberg in the 14th century. When the new, outer wall was finished, the city constructed various public buildings on the base of the old one. These included numerous granaries such as the Mauthalle, Unschlitthaus and the Kaiserstallung.

Grain storage was a precautionary measure that enabled the city council to cope with certain types of crisis and thereby obviate social unrest: the stored grain could be used if there was a drastic rise in the price of grain or Nuremberg was threatened with famine. At such times bread, a staple food, could be made available at a rea-

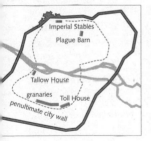

The positions of the municipal granaries in Nuremberg.

sonable price and in sufficient quantity. A typical granary had a large loft area containing many floors. Storage was a costly process, as the grain had to be constantly turned and replaced. A special council deputation was responsible for this. However, time and again the council's foresight paid off because the population was often threatened with inflation and famine. Until well into the 19th century, hunger was a frequent problem for the city.

At the beginning of the 1570s, the municipal toll and weigh-house moved into the large hall on the ground floor of the Mauthalle. Now the city had two weighing houses, the older one being located in Waaggasse. For a long time the Mauthalle was known in Nuremberg as the "Great Scales" or "Superior Scales". Its present-day name first came into use in the 19th century.

61

⑯

St. Clare

Devout Women and a Determined Abbess

The Church of St. Clare is a perfect example of the simplicity associated with churches of medieval mendicant orders. Photo, 2008.

Caritas Pirckheimer, the highly-educated abbess of the Poor Clares' convent and sister of the humanist Willibald Pirckheimer, opposed the Reformation. Posthumous portrait, copperplate engraving by Georg Fenitzer, 17th century.

Charitas Pirck-heimerin Aptiffin in st: Claren Closter. in Nürnberg. Obijt 1532.

■ Cloisters were a prominent feature of medieval Nuremberg. Prior to the Reformation, there were no less than two convents and seven monasteries. All the important orders were represented: Benedictines, Augustinian Hermits, Franciscans, Dominicans, Carthusians, Carmelites and the Teutonic Order. Closely supervised by the city council – sometimes a cause of friction – the orders experienced a cultural boom before the Reformation. For instance, on the evidence available, the Dominican Convent of St. Catherine had the largest convent library in medieval Germany.

St. Clare's Church recalls the Order of St. Clare (Klarissen). Alterations carried out there in 2007 successfully combined medieval architecture with modern ecclesiastical design. Dispensing with a tower, the building's simplicity exemplifies a traditional church of the medieval mendicant orders. The convent complex covered a large area, reaching as far as the city wall. This explains why the gate that leads to the southeast – today part of the Craftsmen's Court (Handwerkerhof) – is called Frauentor (Women's Gate). The city's New Museum has al-

Well into the 19th century the convent of the Poor Clares, which reached to the city wall, remained undeveloped. Section of a coloured copperplate engraving, 1654.

so been built on land formerly occupied by the cloister and so the new square in front of the museum bears the name Klarissenplatz.

Above all, the convent achieved fame through its attitude to the Reformation. The nuns vigorously resisted the policies of the council after it became Lutheran. They were led by the abbess, Caritas Pirckheimer, who saw no reason why the nuns should abandon the life they had freely chosen. She told the reformers that members of the order should be allowed to follow their conscience. Although she could not prevent the eventual demise of the convent and Nuremberg's conversion to Lutheranism, she nevertheless persuaded the council to adopt a more moderate policy: the convent was not closed but was prevented from accepting any more novices, so the community there eventually died out.

Today, the church is once again a place of Catholic worship. In 1854 it was presented to the Catholic community that had re-established itself after 1806. During excavations, a part of Caritas' gravestone was found there. The adjoining house of the Catholic parish church now bears her name.

⑰

A Tour of Nuremberg's Museums

On the Trail of the Imperial City

▌ Those interested in Nuremberg's imperial past are well-served by the city's museums. The largest is the German National Museum, with a vast collection of exhibits relating to the history of art and culture in central Europe. It also pays to visit the Fembohaus City Museum, Albrecht Dürer's House and the Museum Tucher Mansion.

The German National Museum

The museum building itself can be regarded as an exhibit – its core is the former medieval Carthusian monastery, dating from the end of the 14th century. Since 1857 the German National Museum has exhibited its collections here. As a result, the monastery's former church, stations of the cross and the monks' cells are also on display for the visitor.

View of the north wing of the cloister in the former Carthusian monastery.

The museum's medieval section begins with the early period of the Franks in Franconia. Not to be missed here is the splendid binding of the Echternach Missal from the 10th century. Nuremberg artwork makes its first appearance in the section dealing with the late Middle Ages. Outstanding examples are the tapestries from the 14th and 15th centuries. Nuremberg sculptures from the late Gothic period evidence the religious devotion prior to the Reformation. Examples

The so-called "emperor paintings" (Kaiserbilder) by Albrecht Dürer were intended for the relics chamber (Heiltumskammer) in the Schopperhaus on the main market square. The imperial treasure, robes and relics were always brought there the day before being put on public display (Heiltumsweisung). The painting on the left shows Charles the Great, the one on the right Emperor Sigismund, who presented the imperial regalia to Nuremberg in 1423. Oil painting on wood, from around 1512.

here are a palm donkey, which was carried in Palm Sunday processions, and the "Tobias and Rafael" group of sculptures by Veit Stoß. The high altar of the Convent of St. Katherine, with scenes from the life of the saint, is located in the former Carthusian church. The altar paintings date from around 1470 and originate from the workshop of Hans Pleydenwurff. The original stations of the cross by Adam Kraft from the late 15th century have been placed on the walls. This Way of the Cross, with seven stations, led from Gamekeeper's Gate Square to St. John's Cemetery and is one of the oldest surviving of its kind.

The reliquary (Heiltumsschrein) in which the imperial regalia were kept for centuries now hangs in the former sacristy of the Carthusian church. When the regalia were taken to Vienna, the shrine remained in Nuremberg. Visitors to the museum section that contains the stations of the

65

cross should also view in particular the figures from the Beautiful Well, the small gallery (Chörlein) of the Sebaldus rectory and a charming fountain figure "Hansel" from the Hospital of the Holy Spirit. Other interesting exhibits recalling life in the medieval city can be seen in the rooms containing furniture from the Middle Ages.

The museum's collection of paintings contains the few works by Dürer that have remained in Nuremberg: the portraits of the emperors Charles the Great and Sigismund, his mother Barbara Dürer and his teacher, the artist Michael Wolgemut.

Albrecht Dürer's House

⑱

Since the 19th century the house at Gamekeeper's Gate, purchased by Dürer in 1509, has been a Dürer museum, dedicated to preserving the memory of Nuremberg's most famous son. The building is at the same time a good example of a Nuremberg town house of the 15th century. The museum divides up into three thematic zones. The first informs visitors about the history of the house and its inhabitants, paying particular attention to the period from 1509 to 1528, when it was Dürer's workshop and living quarters. Using a multivision show, the second theme concentrates on Dürer the artist. The third part of the museum is dedicated to his workshop. It contains information about the various art techniques and materials employed by artists at the time e.g. the making of pigments, woodcuts and copperplate engravings. A replica of a printing press from the time of Dürer gives the visitor some insight into the method used by Dürer to produce relief prints.

The "Wanderer Room" (Wanderer-Zimmer) in Albrecht Dürer's House. It was built in the late-Renaissance style by the Nuremberg artist Friedrich Wilhelm Wanderer in 1880.

City Museum Fembo House

Fembo House (Fembohaus) is one of the best-preserved town houses in Nuremberg. Its elaborate gable is a distinctive feature – an architectural detail that was actually forbidden in Nuremberg, as houses were not supposed to have their gables facing the street. The building's location on the castle hill made it possible to decorate the gable in this way. Fembo House Museum deals with the history and culture of Nuremberg from the Middle Ages to the 19th century. At the beginning of the museum tour, a wooden model of Nuremberg, in combination with sound and lighting effects, presents in detail the old city as a work of art in itself, one that was lost to the world after WWII.

The next level is dedicated to the cornerstones of Nuremberg's growth in the Middle Ages: loyalty to the emperor, the constitution of the city council, trade and craftsmanship. Exhibits such as the imperial throne from the town hall, the large painting of the main market by Lorenz Strauch and various products that were manufactured in Nuremberg, tell the story of the city's success. The Fembo House dance hall and the "Beautiful

Room" (Schönes Zimmer) from Peller House (Pellerhaus) give some indication of the splendour hidden behind many of the rather sober façades in the city. Joachim Sandrat's large-format painting of the Peace Banquet recalls the days in 1649/50 when Nuremberg once again took centre stage in European politics: a congress in Nuremberg, which lasted over two years, dealt with the unresolved questions of detail relating to the Peace of Westphalia that had been signed in 1648.

The exquisite rooms on the first floor are the work of the Italian stuccoer Donato Polli. They have retained their rococo appearance and provide the setting for the presentation of portraits of important Nuremberg personalities from the 18th century. The changes to the cityscape that took place in the 19th and 20th centuries form the subject of the final part of the exhibition.

Museum Tucher Mansion

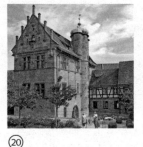

Tucher Mansion (Tucherschloss) is situated in the northeast of the old city, in the middle of an area that was heavily bombed during the war and has since been redeveloped. The Tuchers, an influential patrician family, had a large garden here, and they built a small "palace" on the site in the first half of the 16th century. Today, the building gives an insight into patrician domestic culture from the 16th to the 19th century. The entrance area on the ground floor is impressive, with the large hall covered by cross-ribbed vaulting and its adjoining rooms. The living quarters and representative rooms are to be found on the upper floors. In contrast to the simplicity of the building's outer façade – due to the city council's

View of the restored Hirsvogel's Hall.

strict rule forbidding any external embellishment – the courtyard is truly a Renaissance gem.

In the garden a further jewel from Nuremberg's patrician-culture awaits the visitor: Hirsvogel's Hall (Hirsvogelsaal). The hall's original site, near Tucher Palace, was destroyed in the Second World War. However, various parts of the room, which dates from 1534 and is one of Germany's most famous Renaissance halls, had already been removed and stored elsewhere. These survived the war and were incorporated into the present hall, a true-to-scale reconstruction, in 2000.

For those wishing to spend more time exploring the theme of "patrician domestic culture", a trip to Neunhof in Garlic Land (Knoblauchsland) – an area of Nuremberg where vegetables have been cultivated for centuries – is recommended. The manor house there is a branch museum of the German National Museum.

BIBLIOGRAPHY

BAUER, FRANZ: Alt-Nürnberg. Sagen, Geschichten und Legenden, München [7]1995.

BROCKMANN, STEPHEN: Nuremberg. The Imaginary Capital, Rochester/Woodbridge 2006.

DIEFENBACHER, MICHAEL/ENDRES, RUDOLF (HG.): Stadtlexikon Nürnberg, Nürnberg 1999.

FLEISCHMANN, PETER: Nürnberg mit Fürth und Erlangen. Von der Reichsstadt zur fränkischen Metropole, Köln 1997.

FLEISCHMANN, PETER: Rat und Patriziat in Nürnberg. Die Herrschaft der Ratsgeschlechter vom 13. bis zum 18. Jahrhundert, Nürnberger Forschungen, Band 31, Nürnberg 2008.

FRIEDEL, BIRGIT: Die Nürnberger Burg. Geschichte, Baugeschichte und Archäologie, Petersberg 2007.

GENERALDIREKTION DER STAATLICHEN ARCHIVE BAYERNS (HG.): Nürnberg – Kaiser und Reich. Ausstellung des Staatsarchivs Nürnberg, München 1986.

GERMANISCHES NATIONALMUSEUM (HG.): Nürnberg 1300-1550 – Kunst der Gotik und Renaissance, München 1986.

GESCHICHTE FÜR ALLE E.V. (HG.): Architektur Nürnberg, Bauten und Biographien. Vom Mittelalter bis zum Wiederaufbau, Nürnberg [2]2007.

GRIEB, MANFRED H. (HG.): Nürnberger Künstlerlexikon. Bildende Künstler, Kunsthandwerker, Gelehrte, Sammler, Kulturschaffende und Mäzene vom 12. bis zur Mitte des 20. Jahrhunderts, München 2007.

GROEBNER, VALENTIN: Ökonomie ohne Haus. Zum Wirtschaften armer Leute in Nürnberg am Ende des 15. Jahrhunderts, Göttingen 1993.

IMHOFF, CHRISTOPH VON: Berühmte Nürnberger aus neun Jahrhunderten, Nürnberg [2]1989.

KURRAS, LOTTE/MACHILEK, FRANZ: Caritas Pirckheimer (1467-1532). Ausstellung der kath. Stadtkirche Nürnberg, München 1982.

MAAS, HERBERT: Nürnberg. Geschichte und Geschichten, Nürnberg 1988.

MUSEEN DER STADT NÜRNBERG (HG.): Im Anfang war das Wort. Nürnberg und der Protestantismus, Nürnberg 1996.

OSTERMAYER, VERA: Der Engelsgruß von Veit Stoß in St. Lorenz Nürnberg, Nürnberg 2007.

OSTERMAYER, VERA: Das Sakramentshaus von Adam Kraft in St. Lorenz Nürnberg, Nürnberg 2008.

PFEIFFER, GERHARD: Nürnberg. Geschichte einer europäischen Stadt, München 1971.

REBEL, ERNST: Albrecht Dürer. Maler und Humanist, München 1996.

REICKE, EMIL: Geschichte der Reichsstadt Nürnberg, Nürnberg 1896.

SCHIEBER, MARTIN: Geschichte Nürnbergs, München [2]2007.

SCHIERMEIER, FRANZ: Stadtatlas Nürnberg. Karten und Modelle von 1492 bis heute, Nürnberg 2006.

SCHLEIF, CORINE: Donatio et Memoria. Stifter, Stiftungen und Motivationen an Beispielen der Lorenzkirche in Nürnberg, München 1990.

STRAUSS, GERALD: Nuremberg in the Sixteenth Century. City Politics and Life Between Middle Ages and Modern Times, Bloomington 1976.

STROMER, WOLFGANG VON: Nürnberg als Epizentrum von Erfindungen und Innovationen an der Wende vom Mittelalter zur Neuzeit, in: Schachtschneider, Karl Albrecht (Hg.): Wirtschaft, Gesellschaft und Staat um Umbruch, Berlin 1994.

WEILANDT, GERHARD: Die Sebalduskirche in Nürnberg: Bild und Gesellschaft im Zeitalter der Gotik und Renaissance, Petersberg 2007.

Available in the "Historic Walks" series:

THE NAZI PARTY RALLY GROUNDS IN NUREMBERG
A Short Guide
ISBN 978-3-930699-45-2

THE NUREMBERG TRIALS
A Short Guide
ISBN 978-3-930699-52-0

THE HISTORY OF THE JEWS IN FÜRTH
A Short Guide
ISBN 978-3-930699-61-2
(2010)

STOPPING POINTS

1 **Freiung**
Freiung (Freedom) Area

2 **Burghof**
Castle Courtyard

3 **Kaiserstallung**
Imperial Stables

4 **Vestnertor**
Vestnertor Gate

5 **Am Tiergärtnertor**
At Gamekeeper's Gate

18 **Albrecht-Dürer-Haus**
Albrecht Dürer's House

TOWERS

A **Luginsland**
Luginsland Tower

B **Fünfeckturm**
Five-cornered Tower

C **Sinwellturm**
Sinwell Tower

D **Heidenturm**
Heathen's Tower

E **Walpurgiskapelle**
Walpurgis Chapel

F **Eingang Burggarten**
Entrance to Chapel Gardens

G **Himmelstor**
Heaven's Gate

H **Tiefer Brunnen**
Deep Well

J **Innerer Burghof**
Inner Castle Courtyard

K **Doppelkapelle**
Double Chapel

L **Palas**
Emperor's Great Hall

M **Eingang Burggarten**
Entrance to Chapel Gardens

N **Burggarten**
Chapel Gardens

O **Fazuni-Basteien**
Fazuni Bastions

P **Tiergärtnertor**
Gamekeeper's Gate

Q **Zum Bürgermeistergarten**
To the Mayor's Garden